COLLECTED WORKS OF
A.I. ROZENBLAT

STATISTICAL ANALYSIS OF SHIP SPEED IN WAVES AND THE TROPICS

BY

ANATOLY I. ROZENBLAT

DORRANCE PUBLISHING CO., INC.
PITTSBURGH, PENNSYLVANIA 15222

ISBN # 0-8059-4218-1
Printed in the United States of America

First Printing

For information or to order additional books, please write:
Dorrance Publishing Co., Inc.
643 Smithfield Street
Pittsburgh, Pennsylvania 15222
U.S.A.

DEDICATION

To my lovely children,
Moshe and Inna

CONTENTS

PREFACE TO THE FIRST EDITION

Mathematical statistics, and particularly multiple regression analysis, is widely used in many complex research works of industry and economy (transportation, thermodynamical process, etc.) which demand the big capital expenditures for experimental works.

With the development and widespread use of computers today, the role of statistical methods is obvious because it allows us to collect data and to interpret the data and also to determine the conclusion based upon statistical analysis.

This book is meant to help the reader learn more about multiple regression analysis and its application to marine technology for dry cargo ships sailing in the tropics.

It contains three separate themes and chapters and also shows how to make effective use of statistical methods for research work.

We hope that this book will help you to use its wisdom well.

Our sincere thanks to all.

Anatoly I. Rozenblat
January 1998
Chicago, Illinois
U.S.A.

PART ONE

REGRESSION ANALYSIS OF THE EXHAUST TEMPERATURE FOR THE TWO-STROKE-CYCLE DIESEL ENGINE AND SOME PARAMETERS OF THE RUNNING SHIP IN THE TROPICS

ANATOLY I. ROZENBLAT

1. Introduction and Background

At present there are many marine ships and boats that widely use the two-stroke-cycle diesel engines as they have the advantages over the four-cycle diesel engines (Osbourne, 1944). However, the question of heat density and functional analysis of the exhaust temperature for these engines have not been investigated enough (Whalley, 1992) and (Reader and Hooper, 1983). Some attempts in this question were made by the author (Avallone and Baumeister, 1987) in view of functional analysis of the exhaust temperature in connection with relative load for the two-stroke-cycle diesel engine. These conclusions indicate that, with increasing the relative load (or engine speed), the exhaust temperature accordingly increases, but this regression analysis has the nonlinear relationship.

However, the author of this paper does not agree with such a conclusion and the character of the above-named distribution seeks to investigate in his paper the general questions which are joined with heat density of the two-stroke-cycle diesel engine and exhaust temperature in connection with some of the parameters of a running ship in the tropics such as the seawater temperature, duration in-service of ship, wind speed and direction of wind, ship's speed; and the other parameters.

The author thinks that such functional analysis can discover more widely and accurately the complex problems of heat density and the exhaust temperature, which is more important for the diesel engine because the latter works in difficult conditions such as the running ship in the tropics.

2. The Heat Density of a Working Diesel Engine as the Function of Duration In-Service of a Running Ship in the Tropics

The ship is the complex energetic arrangement consisting of the main diesel engine and some auxiliary mechanisms. It is known that the general index of heat density of a diesel engine is the exhaust temperature. However, the conditions of a working engine in the tropics are very difficult because the exhaust temperature rises considerably with the increase of duration in-service of a running ship. These conclusions are confirmed by statistical results which are shown in Figure 1.

Analysis of Figure 1 shows that the exhaust temperature has an irregular character for the period of a running ship in the tropics.

As indicated in Figure 1, there is a general pattern in the increase of the exhaust temperature of a diesel engine from the starting point of the operation ship and engine. The author admits also that Figure 1 in a generalized view is a typical graph for the different diesel engines where the value marked A can take the different values and characterize the amplitude of deviation for each phase of this irregular changing of the exhaust temperature for the period of operation of a ship in the tropics. And besides, Figure 1 shows that the period of mooring of the ship in harbor or on the open roadstead can characterize the other value which is marked B and has the different values for each phase of this distribution for all periods of operation of a ship in the tropics.

As shown in Figure 1, the function of the exhaust temperature (Y) is the time series model and submits to its laws and rules. These conclusions are confirmed by the data which is shown in Figure 2 in view of the scatter-plot diagram of the exhaust temperature and some average forecasting models for it. Considering a graph at a given exhaust temperature in Figure 2, we see that the six-month actual average temperature submits to the nonlinear regression model and has the three-parameter curve having a minimum but without an inflection; i.e., characterized in a generalized view as quadratic polynomial

$$Y = \alpha + \beta X + \delta X^2 \qquad (1)$$

where $\delta > 0$.

Therefore, it is obvious that the relationship between time in-service of ship (engine) and exhaust temperature is within the curvilinear graph and conforms to the data shown in Figure 2; this graph has the estimating equation

$$\hat{Y}_{p_1} = 547.674 - 11.707\, X_1 + 0.07\, X_1^2 \qquad (2).$$

Table 1 shows the actual and estimated data for the six-month average exhaust temperature conforming to Figure 2.

Table 1
The six-month average exhaust temperature

X_i	Y_i	$\hat{Y}_{p_1}$	$(Y_i - \hat{Y}_{p_1})$	$(Y_i - \hat{Y}_{p_1})^2$
30	408.7	386.846	21.854	477.577
60	142.43	155.428	-12.998	168.955
90	0	41.838	-41.838	1750.423
120	53.47	46.076	7.394	54.673
150	192.6	168.142	24.458	598.210
180	425.20	424.154	1.046	1.094

For the three-month moving average forecast model, the exhaust temperature as shown in Figure 2 has a tendency toward growth in connection with increasing the time in-service of a running ship. The same picture is placed by the other exponential smoothing time series forecasting model for the exhaust temperature at the different smoothing constant ($\alpha = 0.1$ and $\alpha = 0.9$); i.e., the exhaust temperature also rises while increasing the duration in-service of a running ship in the tropics.

On these grounds the author thinks that the increasing of exhaust temperature also is joined with the value of marine growth on the body of the ship for this protracted period of operation of the ship in the tropics. So, analyzing Figure 1 and

Figure 2, the author makes the following conclusions:

a. The exhaust temperature of the diesel engine is the function of duration in-service of a running ship in the tropics.

b. Regression analysis of the exhaust temperature has the non-linear character.

c. The functional model of the exhaust temperature submits to the time series forecasting models with its laws and rules.

d. The character of the average exhaust temperature for all periods of a running ship in the tropics has an irregular component diagram with the multiple of phase and branches.

e. In each branch and phase of this the exhaust temperature graph has placed some definite value in view of amplitude (A) and the value of period (B) of a mooring ship in a harbor or the open roadstead for this transition.

f. The nonlinear character of the changing of the average exhaust temperature versus duration in-service of a running ship (diesel engine) in the tropics presents a generalized view of the typical graph for many marine diesel engines and ships.

g. Tendency and natural laws of changing the exhaust temperature is characteristic also so that the value of it considerably rises when increasing the period of operation of a ship (engine) in the tropics. And this rising of the exhaust temperature is provoked by the marine growth on the body of a ship which also considerably increases with the duration in-service of a ship in the tropics.

h. The average values of the exhaust temperature for the diesel engine are characterized and described in a generalized view as the quadratic polynomial equation view

$$Y = \propto + \beta X + \delta X^2$$

where $\delta > 0$, and this equation will be correct for many marine cargo and passenger ships and boats running in the tropics.

i. So the exhaust temperature in the function of the duration in-service of a running ship submits to the time series forecasting model and for this objective possibility to use the moving average forecast models and single exponential forecasts smoothing line for evaluation of exhaust temperature as a forecasting process for running ships (diesel engines) in the tropics.

j. Analyzing the above-named conclusions, the author thinks that the exhaust temperature from the diesel engine (Y_1) is the function of duration (X_1) in-service of a ship (engine) and this functional model submits to the regression analysis $Y_1 = \varphi (X_1)$ and can be described as the nonlinear character of this relationship.

3. Thermodynamical Aspect of Changing Heat Density for the Diesel Engine in Connection with the Engine Speed

These problems were discussed by the authors (Avallone and Baumenstein, 1987). However, the author of this paper, on the basis of statistical data (observed data $i =$ 183) for the cargo ship deidveit = 10,984 ton and the two-stroke-cycle diesel engine = 8,750 bhp shows that the exhaust temperature has a linear regression function.

So this functional analysis has the view $Y_2 = \varphi_1 (X_2)$. Figure 3 shows a scatter diagram of the engine speed versus exhaust temperature. In view of the fact that the coefficient of correlation shown on Figure 3 between the engine speed and exhaust temperature approaches the value of one $(r = 0.997)$, it may be added to this question that the exhaust temperature submits to the linear regression analysis; i.e., the rising of the engine speed directly or proportionally increases the exhaust temperature from the diesel engine. These relationships can be described in view of regression equation:

$$\hat{Y}_{p_2} = 0.34 + 3.92 \, X_2 \qquad (3).$$

The data of these conclusions are shown in Figure 3 where the good correlation is indicated between the exhaust temperature and engine speed. In view of the fact that the coefficient of determination R^2 indicates that this value is equal to 98.9 percent of the variability in the exhaust temperature (Y_2) so that it may be concluded that a very strong linear relationship has been identified in this regression analysis because all observed data falls perfectly on the fitted regression line $\hat{Y}_{p_2} = 0.34 +$ 3.92 X. And the value with a 90 percent confidence interval on M_{y_2/x_2} as shown in Figure 3 and given for a set of X_2 values in Table 2 indicates the fact that the value X_2 "moves away" from the value $\bar{X}_2^* = 58$; i.e., the length of the confidence intervals increases with the increasing of variable value $\hat{Y}_{p_2}$.

Table 2
Ninety percent confidence intervals for M_{y_2/x_2} for X_2

| X_2 | $\hat{Y}_{p_2}$ | Confidence Interval | | |
		Lower Limit	Upper Limit	Length
20	78.74	38.84	116.64	79.8
40	157.14	117.24	197.04	79.8
$\bar{X}_2^* = 58$	227.7	223.7	231.7	8.00
80	313.3	273.4	353.2	79.8
100	392.3	352.32	432.29	79.97
115	451.14	411.2	491.04	79.84

Figure 4 shows the residual plot for the engine speed using the data shown in Figure 3. The residual encircled in Figure 4 corresponds to the observation Y_2 = 300°C when X_2 = 87 r/min; Y_2 = 345°C when X_2 = 95 r/min and Y_2 = 335°C when X_2 = 94 r/min, which are shown in Figure 3 indicates the fact that the data of these exhaust temperatures fall to the other relative load of the diesel engine. The value of it is equal, 0.2 ÷ 0.3, distinguishing from the data shown in Figure 3 with the relative load 0.4 ÷ 0.6 and also moves off away considerably from the regression line $\hat{Y}_{p_2}$ = 0.34 + 3.92 X_2. So the analysis of Figure 3 and Figure 4 allows the following conclusions:

a.   The thermodynamical relationship has the place between the engine speed and exhaust temperature so that this functional connection submits to the regression linear analysis.

b.   The exhaust temperature and heat density rises accordingly with the increasing relative load (engine speed).

c.   Between engine speed (X_2) and the exhaust temperature (Y_2) for the two-stroke-cycle diesel engine there is the linear regression dependence of view $\hat{Y}_{p_2}$ = 0.34 + 3.92 X_2 so that this regression line has to place 90 percent confidence interval bands for M_{y_2/x_2} for X_2 values.

4.   Influence of the Different External Factors on the Heat Density and the Exhaust Temperature of a Diesel Engine

a.   The heat density of a diesel engine as a complex function of multiple variables.

The author thinks that the seawater temperature functional is joined with the heat density (H_g) of a working diesel engine, and this dependency is the complex function of view $H_g = \psi(Q)$ where Q equals the quantity of heat absorbed by the diesel engine from burning gases in cylinders. As indicated by the author (Osbourne, 1944), the quantity of heat absorbed by the diesel engine can be removed from it 30 to 35 percent by the cooling system with the use of seawater.

So the above-named recommendations mark the fact that is the functional connection between heat absorbed by the diesel engine and seawater temperature (t_w) in view $Q = \varphi(t_w)$. But the quantity of heat absorbed by the diesel engine which is also functional depends on the exhaust temperature (T_g); i.e., this is correct for the function of view $Q = \varphi_1(T_g)$ where the exhaust temperature is also the function of relative load (engine speed); i.e., $T_g = \varphi_2(n)$. Analysis of the dependency of the exhaust temperature in connection with the duration in-service (N) of a running ship in the tropics, as was shown in Figure 2, also admits that the exhaust temperature has the function of view $T_g = \varphi_3(N)$; i.e., the exhaust temperature is the complex function of view $T_g = \varphi_4(n, N)$ or $T_g = \varphi_5\{\varphi_4[\varphi_2(n); \varphi_3(N)]\}$. Therefore, the complex functional model for quantity of heat absorbed by the diesel engine can be impressed in view:

$$Q = \varphi_6 | | \; \varphi_1 \{\varphi_5(\varphi_4[\varphi_2(n); \varphi_3(N)])\}; \varphi(t_w) | | \qquad (4).$$

And for the heat density of the diesel engine this dependency has the following view:

$$H_g = \psi \; [\varphi_6 | | \; \varphi_1 \{\varphi_5(\varphi_4[\varphi_2(n); \varphi_3(N)])\}; \varphi(t_w) | | \;] \quad (5).$$

From the functional equations (4 and 5) we see that the heat density and the exhaust temperature of a diesel engine include such variables as:

n = engine speed (relative load);
t_w = seawater temperature;
N = duration in-service of a running ship (engine) in the tropics.

b. Correlation of the exhaust temperature from a diesel engine and seawater temperature.

As was indicated above, the exhaust temperature (T_g) is the function of relative load (engine speed), and this dependency expresses such an equation as $T_g = \varphi_2(n)$. Such a dependency is confirmed by the data which is shown in Figure 3. However, the exhaust temperature is also the function of seawater temperature; i.e., this dependency has view $T_g = \psi_1(t_w)$ (6). The functional model (6) is confirmed by the data shown in Figure 5 where it is introduced in the scatter-plot diagram of seawater temperature versus exhaust temperature of a diesel engine. Analysis of Figure 5 shows that exhaust temperature has the linear regression character of distribution according to the seawater temperature. Therefore, it can be marked more accurately that the exhaust temperature is the complex functional model of multiple variables and has the following view:

$$T_g = \psi_2 || \varphi_5\{\varphi_4[\varphi_2(n); \varphi_3(N)]\}; \psi_1 (t_w)|| \qquad (7).$$

The data shown in Figure 5 also indicates that these relationships have a linear regression dependency and are characterized with a negative slope. From this functional model (7) and Figure 5 it may be concluded that with a rising seawater temperature (t_w) the exhaust temperature from the diesel engine accordingly decreases. These conclusions are confirmed by the data in Figure 5 for correlation of the exhaust temperature and seawater temperature and is disclosed in view of regression line:

$$\hat{Y}_{p_4} = 1106.436 - 35.387\, X_4 \qquad (8)$$

with estimated data including the standing of the ship (observed data i = 183) and for the regression line of view

$$\hat{Y}^1_{p_4} = 440.552 - 1.228\, X_4 \qquad (9)$$

with estimated data without standing of the ship (observed data i^1 = 92) with some characteristics shown in Figure 5.

At that time the coefficient of determination R^2 for the observed data with i = 183 is equal to 0.44; i.e., R^2 = 0.44, and we see only 44.00 percent of the variability in Y_4. Therefore, there is a middle strength of the linear relationship between the seawater temperature and the exhaust temperature. The worst picture we can see is in Figure 5 with the observed data i = 92, where the coefficient of determination is equal to 0.03; i.e., R^2 = 0.03, so only 3.00 percent of the variability is in Y_4. Estimated 90 percent confidence intervals for M_{y_4/x_4} for the values of seawater temperature are shown in Table 3 for observed data with i = 183.

Table 3
Ninety percent confidence intervals for M_{y_4/x_4} for X_4 values

X_4	$\hat{Y}_{p_4}$	Confidence Interval		
		Lower Limit	Upper Limit	Length
20	398.697	366.36	431.04	64.68
$\bar{X}_4 = 25$	221.757	201.89	241.62	39.73
27	150.990	129.80	172.2	42.4

From Figure 5 and Table 3 we see that the value X_4 "moves away" from the value $\bar{X}_4^1 = 25$, so that with the decreasing of seawater temperature this confidence interval increases considerably. In Table 4 ninety percent confidence intervals are shown for M_{y_4/x_4} for X_4, the values of seawater temperature for the observed data with i^1 = 92 (the ship is only running without standing in harbors).

Table 4
Ninety percent confidence intervals for M_{y_4/x_4} for X_4 values with $i' = 92$.

X_4	$\hat{Y}_{p_4}^{\prime}$	Confidence Interval		
		Lower Limit	Upper Limit	Length
14	423.362	413.07	433.652	20.582
17	419.676	412.27	427.090	14.820
20	415.992	410.992	412.002	10.010
$\bar{X}_4^{\prime} = 25$	409.852	405.28	414.420	9.140

From Figure 5 and Table 4 we see also that the value X_4 "moves away" from the value $\bar{X}_4^{\prime} = 25$ so that with the decreasing of seawater temperature this confidence interval also increases considerably.

Analyzing residual plot for the exhaust temperature ($i = 183$) is shown in Figure 6. We see that residuals of exhaust temperature have two plots. One of them has the mixed residuals as negative at the beginning of the experimental data; at the end of the experiment, the residuals are positive. The other plot has only the negative residuals as these observations certainly lead to the condition that the ship for a long time was standing in the harbor and on the roadstead (about three months) from the total duration of operation of the ship (engine) in the tropics.

On the basis of the above-stated facts and the data of Figure 5 and Figure 6, the author makes the conclusion that between seawater temperature and the exhaust temperature there is the correlation of the linear connection with the negative slope so that the value of slope of this fitted regression line $\hat{Y}_{p4} = 1106.436 - 35.387\ X_4$. It characterizes itself as the observed data with $i = 183$ of the mixed view (the ship is in a regime of transition and standing) considerably larger than the value of slope regression line $\hat{Y}_{p4} = 440.552 - 1.228\ X_4$, characterizing itself as the observed data with $i' = 92$ (the ship is in regime only of transition). The author makes the conclusion that the periodical or long-time standing of the ship in the harbor or on the roadstead positively influences the heat density of a working engine; i.e., with an increase of seawater temperature accordingly decreases for the exhaust temperature from the engine, and this all can be reached by the fact that diesel engines do not operate for a long time in the tropics, particularly on the standing processes with observed data $i = 183$ and the coefficient of determination is equal to $R^2 = 0.44$.

The different pictures are placed with observed data $i' = 92$ (the ship only running), and we see that the coefficient of determination R^2 is equal to $R^2 = 0.03$; i.e., the author thinks this has placed a small correlation between seawater temperature and the exhaust temperature as this is shown in Figure 5 with insignificance negative slope (coefficient b_1 is equal to $b_1 = -1.228$). The conclusion is made by the author about changing engine speed from seawater temperature as shown in Figure 7. This functional analysis shows that with increasing seawater temperature the engine speed considerably decreases, and therefore the author's conclusion is confirmed by the data shown in Figure 5 and Figure 7 because the engine speed and the exhaust temperature are joined functionally.

c. Influence by the other operational parameters of a running ship (wind speed and its direction, ship's speed, etc.) on the character of changing exhaust temperature from diesel engine.

As was indicated in the above-stated conclusion, the exhaust temperature from the diesel engine is a function depending on multiple factors such as relative load (engine speed), duration in-service of a running ship, or marine growth of body ship, and also the seawater temperature. But examining more attentively the other operational parameters of a running ship, the author makes the conclusion, on the basis of data in Figure 8, where it shows scatter plots of wind speed versus the exhaust temperature illustrating that the functional relationship is absent between the above-named parameters as the regression line is perfectly horizontal, as illustrated in Figure 8. Therefore, the value of the coefficient is equal to $b_1 = 0$ and the regression line is equal to $\hat{Y}_{P_7} = 412.47 + OX_7$ (10). So, the author thinks that exhaust temperature does not depend on the wind speed and its direction in the process of a running ship in the tropics; i.e., the correlation between these values is absent.

These conclusions are confirmed by the data illustrated in Figure 9, where shown also are scatter plots of the direction of wind on the body of a ship versus the exhaust temperature, and this dependence is marked by the regression line in view $\hat{Y}_{P_8} = 412.47 + OX_8$ (11). The functional analysis of ship speed and exhaust temperature can be expressed by the dependency of view $Y_9 = \varphi(X_9)$.

As shown in Figure 10, this correlation between the above-stated parameters is marked in view of a scatter plot and the fitted regression line has view $\hat{Y}_{P_9} = 473.43 - 4.41 X_9$ (12) for the exhaust temperature. In view of the fact that the coefficient b_1 of this regression line (12) is the negative ($b_1 = -4.41$), this indicates the fact that the regression line decreases as the value of ship speed X_9 increases. Analysis of this function is graphed in Figure 10. The author admits that with the increasing of ship speed, the exhaust temperature accordingly decreases, and this may be explained by the fact that with increasing ship speed, the value of marine growth on the body of the ship considerably decreases; i.e., accordingly the movement-resistance coefficient also decreases. Therefore, both of these above-named factors improve the work of the diesel engine on account of decreasing heat density and exhaust temperature in the operation processes of both the ship and engine in the tropics. This functional connection can be expressed as $X_9 = \varphi_1 (X_{10}; X_{11})$, where X_{10} equals the value of marine growth on the body of the ship; X_{11} equals the movement-resistance coefficient and as the above-stated $X_9 = \varphi_2 (n)$, where n equals engine speed (or relative load).

So this functional model has view:

$$X_9 = \varphi_3 [\varphi_1(X_{10}; X_{11}); \varphi_2(n)]$$

and then

$$Y_9 = \varphi_4||\varphi\{\varphi_3[\varphi_1(X_{10}; X_{11}); \varphi_2(n)]\}|| \qquad (13)$$

or

$$T_g = \varphi_4||\varphi\{\varphi_3[\varphi_1(X_{10}; X_{11}); \varphi_2(n)]\}|| \qquad (13a).$$

On the basis of the above-stated views, the author thinks that the ship's speed indirectly influences the exhaust temperature, although we do not see the strength of the linear relationship between the independent variable X_9 (ship's speed) and dependent variable Y_9 (exhaust temperature) because the coefficient of determination R^2 is very small and its value is equal to $R^2 = 0.07$. Functionally the engine speed has more influence on the ship's speed. Besides, the author indicates the fact that the increasing of ship speed promotes the decreasing level of marine growth on the body of the ship and therefore also promotes the decreasing of exhaust temperature from diesel engine and of its heat density.

5. Conclusion and Recommendations

Considering the regression analysis of exhaust temperature for the two-stroke-cycle diesel engine, the author makes the conclusion that this dependent variable is the complex function of many multiple independent variables such as:

a. Engine speed (or relative load) appears as a general thermodynamical parameter changing the heat density and exhaust temperature of a working diesel engine.

b. External factors indirectly appear on the character of changing temperature such as:
    (1) duration in-service of a running ship (or marine growth on its body);
    (2) seawater temperature;
    (3) ship's speed.

c. The author in his paper indicates the fact that between engine speed and exhaust temperature has placed the correlation in the view of a linear regression line. And we see that with the rising of ship speed, the exhaust temperature considerably decreases and improves the conditions of heat density of the diesel engine; i.e., it accordingly increases its service life because, in this period of running the ship, the level of marine growth on its body is insignificant.

d. And besides we see also that the changing of the average exhaust temperature connected to the in-service duration of a running ship submits to the quadratic polynomial equation of view $Y = \propto + \beta X + \delta X^2$ ($\delta > 0$), and the exhaust temperature for this operation period is characterized as increasing; i.e., with the rising of the duration in-service of a running ship the exhaust temperature of the diesel engine accordingly increases.

e. The author also admits that between wind speed and its direction and also exhaust temperature of diesel engine the correlation is absent.

f. In this paper the author also indicates the fact that engine speed and exhaust temperature decrease with increasing seawater tempera-ture because the above-named factors are joined functionally with the seawater temperature.

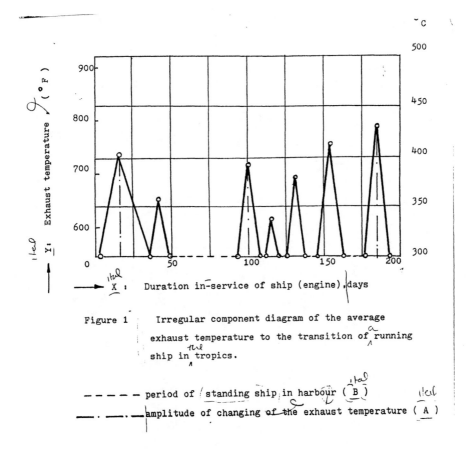

Figure 1   Irregular component diagram of the average
exhaust temperature to the transition of running
ship in tropics.

- - - - - period of standing ship in harbour (B)

—.—.— amplitude of changing of the exhaust temperature (A)

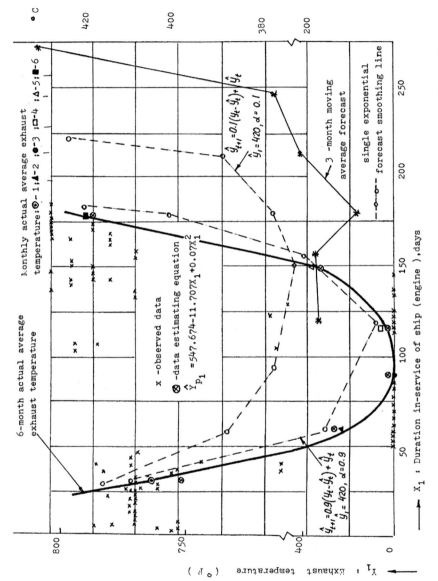

Figure 2   Scatter plot diagram of the exhaust temperature and some average forecasting
models for it

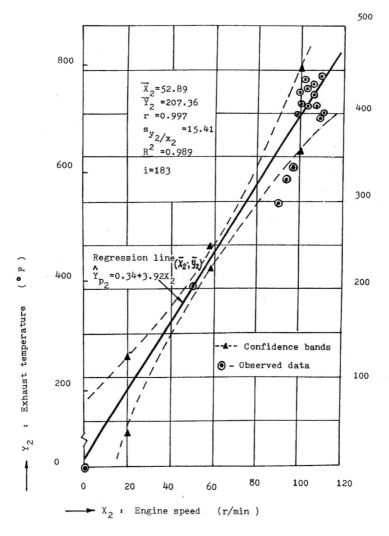

Figure 3 Scatter diagram of engine speed versus
of exhaust temperature

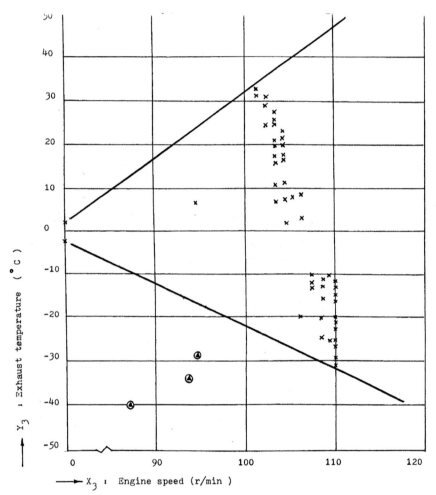

Figure 4 Residual plot of data shown on Figure 1

x - observed data with relative load (0.4 ÷0.6)

⊕ - observed data with relative load (0.2 ÷ 0.3) [2]

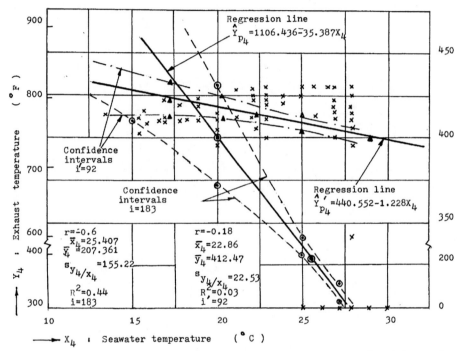

Figure 5   Scatter plot of seawater temperature versus exhaust temperatur

x   - observed data

——⊙————⊙——— -estimated data including standing of ship (i =183)

——▲————▲—— - estimated data without standing of ship (i′=92)

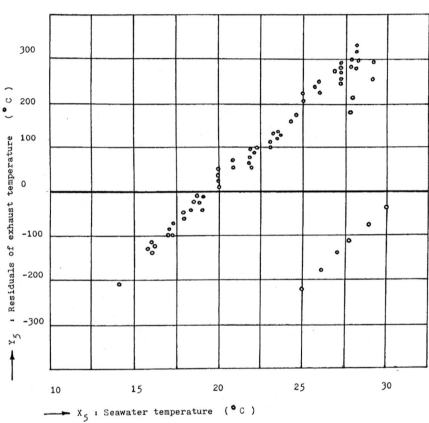

Figure 6 Residual plot for the exhaust temperature (i=183)

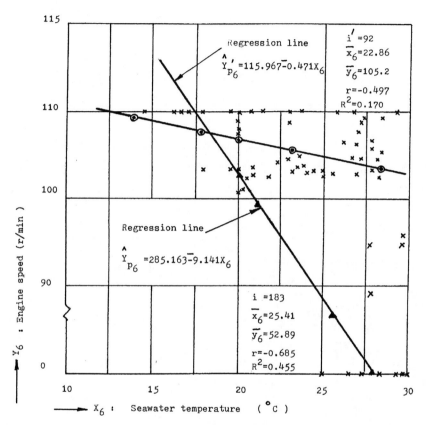

Figure 7 Scatter plot of seawater temperature versus of engine
speed and some regression lines.

x -observed data

⊚ regression line without standing ship in harbors;

▲ regression line with the standing ship in harbors.

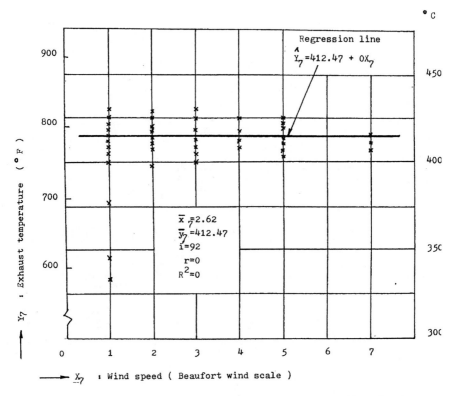

Figure 8 Scatter plot of wind speed versus   the exhaust
temperature from diesel engine

x -observed data

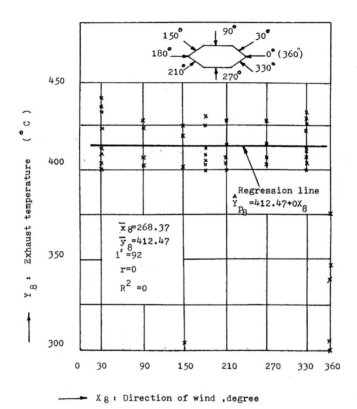

Figure 9 Scatter plot of direction of wind versus the exhaust temperature

x - observed data

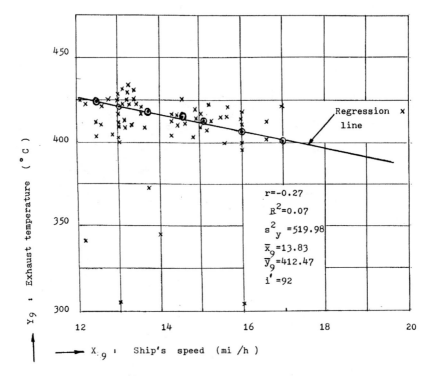

Figure 10 Scatter plot and fitted regression line
$\hat{Y}_{P_9}$ =473.43 -4.41X_9 for the exhaust temperature
of diesel engine

x - observed data

References

1. Osbourne, *Modern Marine Engineer's Manual*, (New York: Cornell Maritime Press, 1944), 2: 15-15, 15-243.

2. P. B. Whalley, *Basic Engineering Thermodynamics*, (New York: Oxford University Press, 1992): 203-205.

3. G.T. Reader and C. Hooper, *Stirling Engineer*, (London: E. & F. N. Spon., 1983): 88-89.

4. Eugene A. Avallone and Theodore Baumeister III, *Mark's Standard Handbook for Mechanical Engineers*, (New York: McGraw-Hill Book Company, 1987): 9-112.

Bibliography

Bowerman, Bruce L. and O'Connell, Richard T., *Time Series and Forecasting*. North Scituate, Massachusetts: Duxbury Press, 1979.

Croxton, Frederick E. and Cowden, Dudley J., *Applied General Statistics*. New York: Prentice-Hall, Inc., 1939.

Pfaffenberg, Roger C. and Patterson, James H., *Statistical Methods*. Homewood, Illinois: Richard D. Irwin, Inc., 1977.

Ratkowsky, David A., *Handbook of Nonlinear Regression Models*. New York: Marcel Dekker, Inc., 1990.

PART TWO

STATISTICAL ANALYSIS OF SHIP SPEED IN THE TROPICS

1. Introduction and Background

The statistical methods used vary widely in the evaluation of different problems in marine engineering by the author (Perakis, 1991). However they will be used in regard to the questions of studying ship speed, possibly to relate only the information of the data of which was investigated on the basis of using a merchant vehicle in the conditions of the Caspian and Baltic Seas (Zvonkov, 1956). This paper also marks that the reduction of ship speed is the function of a duration in-service of a ship and this dependence has a nonlinear character. The conclusions of the author do not consider the questions of the ship speed reduction and does not take into account the ship standing in the ports or on the roadstead.

Some attempts of analysis of the ship speed was made by the author (Parker, 1971) and (Lacey and Edwards, 1993), but their concerns are mainly the conditions of sailing ships in cold seawaters. Considering the above-named factors, the author of this paper thinks that the questions of the ship speed reduction in the conditions of a sailing ship in the tropics are of considerable interest for the seaman and navigational services.

2. The Advantages of Statistical Methods in the Evaluation of the Ship Speed

The most important factor in the evaluation of total cost of transportation of commercial cargos by sea is the ship speed (Avallone and Baumenstein, 1987). However, this index is the complex function which depends on multiple independent variables and submits to the law of occasional values. Naturally receiving reliable statistical data on the real object-merchant vehicle is of the most value and most important to the research worker because it does not demand considerable capital investment on realization or expensive laboratory investigation, for example, testing in a special pool, and besides, everything increases in the future of the range of using statistical methods in industrial conditions.

On the basis of the above-named circumstances, the author in his paper thinks that correlation analysis, as one of the varieties of the statistical method in the evaluation of the ship speed, is optimum and the most rational. The general objective of statistical analysis in this paper was to evaluate the ship speed in dependency of such areas as service diesel engine (engine speed, exhaust gas temperature, etc.), voyage duration of merchant vehicle, seawater temperature, and seaway, taking into account the sailing ship in the tropics.

3. Presentation and Analysis of the Statistical Data

The statistical data of analysis are included in view of tables in Appendix 1 and are considered for the merchant vehicle having the following characteristics:

    a.   Deidveit = 10,984 ton;

b.   Type of marine diesel engine = two-stroke-cycle;

c.   Horsepower of diesel engine = 8,750;

d.   Average ship speed = 14.25 knots;

e.   Electrocapacity = 3,700 Kw;

f.   Running area: (Black Sea-Indian Ocean and other tropical seas).

The author, on the basis of the statistical data with the number of observation $N = 183$, attempts to determine the relationship in view of linear and nonlinear correlations between the two variables. In the case of examining an independent variable, one of the parameters of this dependence is used as:

X_1 =   wind direction on the east (E), degree;

X_2 =   wind direction on northeast (NE), degree;

X_3 =   wind direction on north (N), degree;

X_4 =   wind direction on northwest (NW), degree;

X_5 =   wind direction on west (W), degree;

X_6 =   wind direction on southwest (SW), degree;

X_7 =   wind direction on south (S), degree;

X_8 =   wind direction on southeast (SE), degree;

X_9 =   revolution per minute of the main engine;

X_{10} =   duration in-service time of ship, days;

X_{11} =   seawater temperature, °C;

X_{12} =   wind speed (Beaufort wind scale);

X_{13} =   exhaust gas temperature, °C;

and dependent variable was chosen the value as:

Y =   ship speed, miles per hour.

So the author in this paper investigates the following correlation dependencies such as:

$$Y_1 = \varphi_1 (X_1);$$
$$Y_2 = \varphi_2 (X_2);$$
$$Y_3 = \varphi_3 (X_3);$$
$$\dots\dots\dots\dots\dots$$
$$Y_{13} = \varphi_{13} (X_{13}),$$

which will be discussed in the section titled "Discussion and Results." This portion takes into account the peculiarities of the sailing merchant vehicle in the tropics.

4. The Peculiarities of the Sailing Ship in the Tropics

The analysis of sailing ships in the tropics in comparison with the other conditions of sailing has some peculiarities such as:

a. For this ship one observes the intensive marine growth (fouling) in the period of voyage, and accordingly this factor decreases the quick-maneuvering qualities of the ship as a whole.

b. The main marine diesel engine works in more critical conditions (very often have the place overheat and overload of diesel), and naturally these factors decrease the service life of the marine diesel engine as a whole.

c. The total price of transportation of cargo increases as a result of ship speed reduction, which is joined with the duration of service for a ship; i.e., with an increase in quantity of the moorings in ports and duration of service, the ship speed decreases considerably.

d. For some objective reasons (such as the sailing ship in the tropics and the presence of the seaway), the unfavorable conditions on the examined object arise—of the ship, main marine diesel engine, crew, cargo—and we see that all of these component parts are joined between you and the defined laws and demand the complex investigation.

5. Discussion and Results

Using the data given in Appendix 1, we see on Figure 1.1 that the correlation between ship speed and engine speed as shown in view of function $Y_9 = \varphi_9 (X_9)$ has the linear relationship with regression line

$$\hat{V} = 0.07 + 0.13 \, n \qquad (1)$$

with the following summary statistical characteristics:

*average engine speed	$\bar{n} = 52.89$ revolutions per minute;
*average ship speed	$\bar{v} = 6.95$ miles per hour;
*coefficient correlation	$r = 0.992$;
*variance	$s_{v/n} = 1.29$.

Figure 1.1 shows also that with increasing engine speed the ship speed increases accordingly; i.e., this function has the directly proportional dependence. However, a scatter-plot diagram of the duration in-service versus ship speed shown in Figure 1.2 indicates that the correlation between ship speed and duration in-service of a ship shown in view of function $Y_{10} = \varphi_{10}(X_{10})$ has the nonlinear relationship with two curves and regression functions such as:

$$\hat{V}_1 = 16.15N^{-0.02973} \qquad (2)$$

and

$$\hat{V}_2 = 17.36N^{-0.0568} \qquad (3).$$

The first curve with the function $\hat{V}_1 = 16.15N^{0.02973}$ characterizes the first period of the sailing ship (without stopping in ports). And the second curve with the function $\hat{V}_2 = 17.36N^{-0.0568}$ characterizes also the second period of the sailing ship (but already with the ship stopping in ports).

As shown in Figure 1.2, the duration of a ship standing in ports with the tropical climate for more than eighty days and the ship speed at this occasion accordingly decreases in comparison with the first pass of a ship (without stopping). The nonlinear regression line on the first pass with $\hat{V}_1 = 16.15N^{0.02973}$ has the following summary statistical characteristics:

*average duration in-service of ship	$\bar{N}_1 = 21$ days;
*average ship speed	$\hat{V}_1 = 14.89$ miles per hour;
*variance	$\sigma_1 = 0.038$;
*coefficient correlation	$r_1 = 0.28$.

The other nonlinear regression line on the second pass with $\hat{V}_2 = 17.36N^{0.0568}$ has the following summary statistical characteristics:

*average duration in-service of ship	$\bar{N}_2 = 163.5$ days;
*average ship speed	$\hat{V}_2 = 12.99$ mph;
*variance	$\sigma_2 = 0.006$;
*coefficient correlation	$r_2 = 0.25$.

So analysis of Figure 1.2 shows as a whole that, with an increase in the duration in-service of the ship, the ship speed considerably decreases as a result of marine fouling on the body of the ship and which is aggravated with an increase in the time of the ship standing in ports at the loading-unloading operations, particularly in the tropics.

It is necessary to admit that the seawater temperature has a considerable influence on the character of a change in the ship speed, and this fact is confirmed by the conclusions of Figure 1.2 in accordance with the function of $Y_{11} = \varphi_{11}(X_{11})$. However, as Figure 1.3 shows, the value of changes in the ship speed depends also on the character of the location of the ship in seawater. At the mooring of a ship in the tropics (shown by a continuous line) the ship speed has the linear regression line $\hat{V}_1 = 41\text{-}1.34\,T_w$ (4) with the following summary statistical characteristics:

*average seawater temperature	$T_{w_1} = 25.41\,°C;$
*average ship speed	$\hat{V}_1 = 6.95$ miles per hour;
*coefficient correlation	$r_1 = -0.67;$
*coefficient of determination	$R_1^2 = 0.76.$

And at the absence of mooring for a ship in the tropics (as shown by the dash line) the ship speed has the linear regression line $\hat{V}_2 = 15.61\text{-}0.04\,T_w$ (5). So analysis of Figure 1.3 shows that, with increasing seawater temperature, the ship speed abruptly decreases, particularly with an increase in the mooring of a ship in ports or on the roadstead.

No less important question in analysis of ship speed in the tropics, besides the above-named factors, is the seaway factor. So the data indicated in Figure 1.4 shows that, besides the effects of wind speed on the ship speed, the direction of wind, which acts directly on the body of ship in the period of its motion, also has a considerable influence.

From Figure 1.4 we see that the changing ship speed has the linear regression analysis for any direction of wind with the variable parameters of wind speed. In Table 1 are shown the summary characteristics of the wind speed (W_s) versus ship's speed (V) and evaluated for each view of the direction of the wind, having the linear regression lines. As shown in Figure 1.4 with the direction (X_5) of wind to the stern of the ship, the ship's speed considerably increases and then accordingly is larger than the value of wind speed (W_s); that larger number is the ship's speed. However, the reduction of ship speed has a place also at the direction of wind X_2 and X_8, and the ship's speed particularly decreases with the rising wind speed.

So the presence of direction X_5 of the wind to the stern of the ship promotes the acceleration of motion in the ship even at the presence of fouling on the body of a ship in the tropics, and, besides, the above-named conditions considerably improve the regime of service of the main diesel engine.

Figure 1.5 shows the scatter plot of exhaust gas temperature versus ship's speed. Exhaust gas temperature indirectly influences the ship speed, and from Figure 1.5 we see that the changing of this functional dependence $Y_{13} = \varphi(X_{13})$ has the linear regression line $\hat{V} = 18.799\text{-}0.012\,T_g$ (6) with the following summary statistical parameters:

*average engine speed	$\bar{n} = 92$ revolutions per minute;
*average exhaust gas temperature	$\bar{T}_g = 412.47°C$;
*average ship speed	$\bar{V} = 13.83$ miles per hour;
*coefficient correlation	$r = -0.23$;
*coefficient of determination	$R^2 = 0.2$.

From Figure 1.5 we see that with the decreasing exhaust gas temperature; i.e., the engine speed, the ship speed considerably decreases.

Analyzing the multiple regression analysis for the ship speed depends on some variables such as X_9, X_{11}, and X_{13}. We see from Figure 1.6, taken as the base for calculation of nomogram, that the ship's speed in the tropics has the linear regression line and is expressed by the formula:

$$\hat{V}_c = -0.7803 + 0.233X_9 - 0.0256X_{13} + 0.0283X_{11} \qquad \text{(7) or}$$
$$\hat{V}_c = -0.7803 + 0.233n - 0.0256\,T_g + 0.0283\,t_w \qquad \text{(7a).}$$

As the nomogram from Figure 1.6 testifies, having the values such as engine speed (n), exhaust gas temperature (T_g), and the seawater temperature (t_w), we can evaluate the ship speed with precision to 0.5 percent. So at the data $t_w = 22°C$, $n_4 = 110$ rpm, $T_{g_1} = 400°C$ from the nomogram in Figure 1.6, we have $\hat{V}_c = 15.3$ mph. The ship speed calculated on the formula (7a) has the value $\hat{V}_c = 15.23$ mph; i.e., relative error is equal to 0.5 percent.

Table 2 shows the average characteristics of changing the parameters of ship speed $\bar{V}_c$, the seawater temperature $\bar{t}_w$, revolution per minute of the main engine (engine speed) $\bar{n}$, and exhaust gas temperature $\bar{T}_g$ depending on duration of in-service time of a ship in the tropics. The data from Figure 1.7 and Table 2 shows that the most maximal seawater temperature has a place in the middle period of a ship sailing in the tropics (duration of in-service time of a ship is equal to 3, and the seawater temperature is equal to $\bar{t}_w = 28.2°C$. Besides, the values $\bar{n}$, $\bar{T}_g$, and $\bar{V}_c$ at this period of a ship sailing in the tropics have the minimal values ($\bar{V}_c = 0$; $\bar{n} = 0$; $\bar{T}_g = 0$); i.e., the ship at this period was standing, and naturally all of these factors accelerated with the fouling on the body of the ship at this period.

On the basis of this data, the author makes the conclusion that after the long standing time of a ship in the tropics, all parameters of the ship, particularly the engine speed, become worse; i.e., the considerable reduction of the ship speed is observed for the next period of sailing in the tropics.

Table 1
Summary characteristics of the wind speed (W_s) versus ship's speed (V)

Wind direction degree		Estimated regression line	Observed data	Statistical characteristics: Arithmetic mean		Correlation coefficient	Coefficient of determination
Name	Designation	Ship Speed V_1		Wind Speed W_s	Ship's Speed V	r	R^2
East (0)	X_1	$V_1 = 13.23 + 0.35W_s$	41	1.39	13.71	0.28	0.28
Northeast (30)	X_2	$V_2 = 13.64 + 0.03W_s$	9	3.11	13.73	0.13	0.05
North (90)	X_3	$V_3 = 11.36 + 0.63W_s$	6	3.33	13.42	0.93	0.93
Northwest (150)	X_4	$V_4 = 13.04 + 0.297W_s$	4	4.75	14.45	0.35	0.35
West (180)	X_5	$V_5 = 10.21 + 1.81W_s$	6	2.67	15.05	0.51	0.51
Southwest (210)	X_6	$V_6 = 14.69 + 0.05W_s$	5	3.60	14.87	0.04	0.04
South (270)	X_7	$V_7 = 12.02 + 0.35W_s$	9	4.11	13.44	0.83	0.83
Southeast (330)	X_8	$V_8 = 12.83 + 0.18W_s$	12	3.75	13.50	0.49	0.43

Table 2
Average observed data for the merchant ship sailing in the tropics

Duration of service time of ship, months	Ship's speed V_c mi/h	Sea water t_w, °C	Engine speed n r/min	Exhaust gas temperature T_g, °C
1	14.91	19.57	109.7	408.7
2	5.43	27.93	38.20	142.43
3	0	28.20	0	0
4	1.70	20.53	13.73	53.47
5	6.10	26.87	47.73	192.57
6	12.96	22.68	102.94	425.21

6. Conclusions and Recommendations

Analyzing the reduction of ship speed for the merchant vehicle in the conditions of sailing in the tropics, the author of this paper makes the following conclusions:

a. At the beginning of a ship's sailing in the tropics, the reduction of ship speed observed averages 30 percent in comparison to the starting speed.

b. The ship speed is joined functionally to many variable values such as:

*revolution per minute of the main engine (engine speed);
*exhaust gas temperature;
*seawater temperature;
*wind speed;
*direction of wind;
*duration of in-service time of ship.

But the most important factor in the question of reduction of ship speed is the duration of in-service time of a ship, particularly in the tropics, which also indirectly influences the other parameters of the main diesel engine (engine speed, exhaust gas temperature, etc.).

c. The reduction of ship speed is considerable for the tropics, and this negative factor influences the increase of the total price of transportation for the commercial cargos by the maritime way to many countries (India, New Zealand, etc.) with the same tropical climate.

d. The correlation analysis of the change in the ship speed from some independent parameters such as engine speed, seawater temperature, exhaust gas temperature, and parameters of the seaway (wind speed and direction) shows that this dependence has the linear regression model.

e. The correlation analysis of the change in the ship speed from an independent parameter such as the duration of in-service time of a ship has the nonlinear regression model.

f. One index for decreasing the fouling on the body of the ship is reducing the quantity of mooring time for a ship in ports or on the roadstead, particularly in the tropics.

g. An increase in the exhaust gas temperature of the main diesel engine in a period of a ship sailing in the tropics is the first characteristic of the presence of fouling on the body of a ship.

Appendix 1
Statistical Data for Estimating Ship Speed Ÿ

X_1	X_2	X_3	X_4	X_5	X_6	X_7	X_8	X_9	X_{10}	X_{11}	X_{12}	X_{13}	Y
360								110	1	23	1	400	16.4
360								110	2	23	3	400	16.08
							330	110	3	22	3	405	12.5
360								110	4	20	1	400	15.62
				180				110	5	19	4	415	19.85
					210			110	6	17	5	420	16.93
360								110	7	27	1	410	15.93
360								110	8	26	1	410	15.44
							330	110	9	26	7	410	14.83
360								110	10	22	2	410	12.83
360								110	11	22	5	412	14.35
360								110	12	21	5	412	14.78
360								110	13	20	4	411	14.70
	30							110	14	17	1	411	15.80
	30							110	15	16	3	412	15.18
						270		110	16	14	7	410	14.35
	30							110	17	14	7	410	14.50
360								110	18	18	1	415	15.62
					210			110	19	16	3	408	14.60
		90						110	20	16	5	401	14.73
			150					110	21	17	7	407	15.23
				180				110	22	16	3	405	15.30
		90						110	23	17	2	409	12.63
	30							110	24	18	5	408	13.65
							330	110	25	18	4	408	14.55
							330	110	26	19	3	412	14.85
							330	108	27	20	7	405	14.30
							330	107	28	20	7	405	12.95
						270		108	29	20	5	410	14.45
						270		108	30	23	7	410	14.58
360								108	31	27	3	408	14.48
	30							109	32	28	5	403	12.85
360								108	33	27	1	400	12.93
				180				109	34	27	2	417	15.65
					210			108	35	27	5	412	13.60
				180				110	36	28	2	418	15.16
								0	37	28		0	0
					210			106	38	28	2	395	16.10
			150					87	39	28	4	300	16.10
360								87	40	28	1	300	13.43

**Appendix 1
(continued)**

X_1	X_2	X_3	X_4	X_5	X_6	X_7	X_8	X_9	X_{10}	X_{11}	X_{12}	X_{13}	Y
360								107	41	28	1	412	16.55
360								107	42	28	1	408	16.13
								0	43	28		0	0
								0	44	28		0	0
								0	45	28		0	0
								0	46	28		0	0
								0	47	28		0	0
								0	48	28		0	0
								0	49	28		0	0
								0	50	29		0	0
								0	51	29		0	0
								0	52	28		0	0
								0	53	28		0	0
								0	54	28		0	0
								0	55	28		0	0
								0	56	28		0	0
								0	57	28		0	0
								0	58	28		0	0
								0	59	28		0	0
								0	60	28		0	0
								0	61	28		0	0
								0	62	28		0	0
								0	63	28		0	0
								0	64	29		0	0
								0	65	29		0	0
								0	66	29		0	0
								0	67	29		0	0
								0	68	29		0	0
								0	69	29		0	0
								0	70	29		0	0
								0	71	29		0	0
								0	72	29		0	0
								0	73	29		0	0
								0	74	29		0	0
								0	75	28		0	0
								0	76	28		0	0
								0	77	28		0	0
								0	78	28		0	0
								0	79	28		0	0
								0	80	29		0	0

Appendix 1
(continued)

X_1	X_2	X_3	X_4	X_5	X_6	X_7	X_8	X_9	X_{10}	X_{11}	X_{12}	X_{13}	Y
								0	81	29		0	0
								0	82	29		0	0
								0	83	29		0	0
								0	84	29		0	0
								0	85	29		0	0
								0	86	29		0	0
								0	87	25		0	0
								0	88	25		0	0
								0	89	25		0	0
								0	90	25		0	0
								0	91	26		0	0
								0	92	26		0	0
								0	93	26		0	0
								0	94	26		0	0
								0	95	26		0	0
								0	96	26		0	0
								0	97	26		0	0
								0	98	26		0	0
								0	99	26		0	0
								0	100	26		0	0
		90						106	101	27	5	425	14.50
			150					106	102	28	5	419	13.38
				180				106	103	28	3	425	11.23
360								94	104	28	1	335	12.00
								0	105	28		0	0
								0	106	28		0	0
								0	107	28		0	0
								0	108	28		0	0
								0	109	28		0	0
								0	110	29		0	0
								0	111	29		0	0
								0	112	29		0	0
								0	113	28		0	0
								0	114	28		0	0
								0	115	28		0	0
								0	116	28		0	0
								0	117	28		0	0
								0	118	28		0	0
								0	119	29		0	0
								0	120	29		0	0

Appendix 1
(continued)

X_1	X_2	X_3	X_4	X_5	X_6	X_7	X_8	X_9	X_{10}	X_{11}	X_{12}	X_{13}	Y
								0	121	29		0	0
360								95	122	29	1	345	13.75
								0	123	30		0	0
								0	124	28		0	0
								0	125	28		0	0
								0	126	29		0	0
								0	127	29		0	0
								0	128	30		0	0
360								94	129	29	1	375	13.6
360								104	130	26	1	410	13.03
								0	131	28		0	0
								0	132	28		0	0
								0	133	27		0	0
								0	134	27		0	0
360								104	135	28	1	410	13.30
360								102	136	28	1	430	13.30
360								104	137	28	1	425	12.15
360								103	138	27	1	425	11.7
								0	139	28		0	0
								0	140	28		0	0
								0	141	28		0	0
								0	142	28		0	0
								0	143	28		0	0
360								104	144	23	1	415	12.98
360								104	145	23	1	430	13.35
360								104	146	22	1	420	13.13
360								103	147	23	1	420	13.35
360								105	148	23	1	420	13.35
360								103	149	22	1	426	13.03
360								103	150	22	1	426	13.03
	30							103	151	22	1	426	13.03
							330	103	152	22	1	426	13.03
						270		103	153	18.5	2	410	13.23
	30							103	154	19	2	410	12.63
						270		103	155	19	3	415	12.63
360								103	156	19	1	415	12.63
360								103	157	19	1	415	12.63
360								103	158	19	1	420	12.63
360								103	159	24	1	420	12.63
							330	103	160	25	3	425	13.15

Appendix 1
(continued)

X_1	X_2	X_3	X_4	X_5	X_6	X_7	X_8	X_9	X_{10}	X_{11}	X_{12}	X_{13}	Y
							330	103	161	26	2	430	13.10
360								103	162	27	1	430	13.05
360								103	163	28	1	430	13.10
							330	103	164	28	1	425	13.10
	30							103	165	28	2	425	13.15
						270		103	166	25	3	430	13.15
360								103	167	25	1	430	13.10
360								103	168	25	1	425	13.15
				180				103	169	25	2	430	13.10
							330	103	170	24	3	425	13.05
		90						103	171	23	2	430	13.10
							330	104	172	23	4	425	13.15
				210				104	173	23	3	430	13.10
			150					102	174	22	3	425	13.10
360								102	175	22	1	425	13.10
360								103	176	22	1	425	12.90
360								104	177	22	1	430	12.90
						270		103	178	21	4	430	12.90
						270		102	179	21	4	430	12.90
		90						101	180	21	3	430	12.90
		90						105	181	21	3	430	12.80
						270		101	182	20	2	430	12.80
	30							103	183	20	2	430	12.80

Figure 1.1 Scatter plot of engine speed (n) versus ship's speed (v)

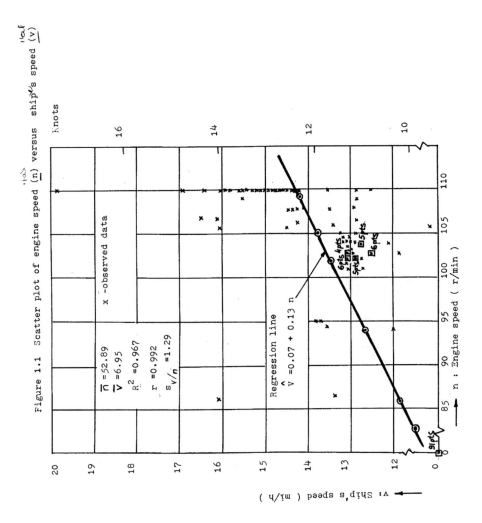

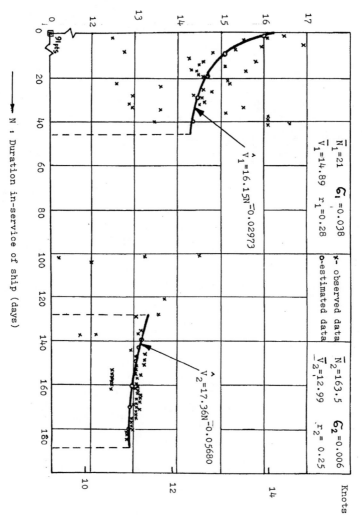

FIGURE 1.2 Scatter plot of duration in-service (N) versus ship's speed(V)

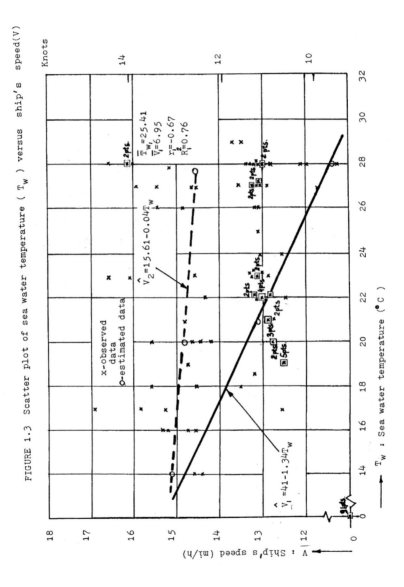

FIGURE 1.3 Scatter plot of sea water temperature (T_w) versus ship's speed(V)

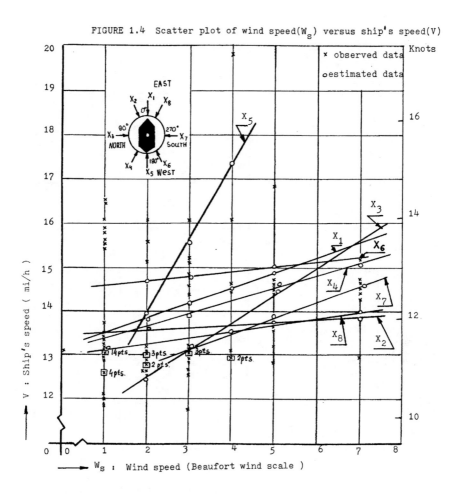

FIGURE 1.4 Scatter plot of wind speed(W_s) versus ship's speed(V)

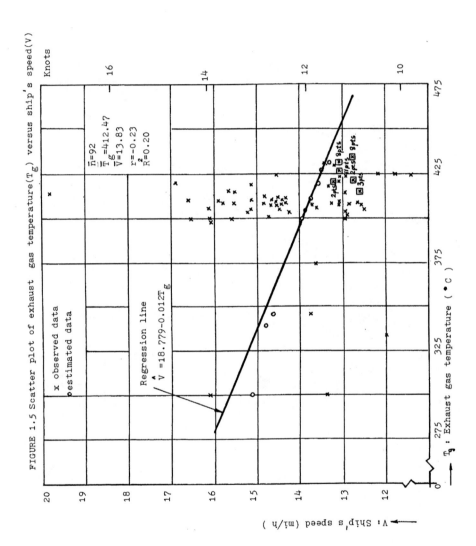

FIGURE 1.5 Scatter plot of exhaust gas temperature(T_g) versus ship's speed(V)

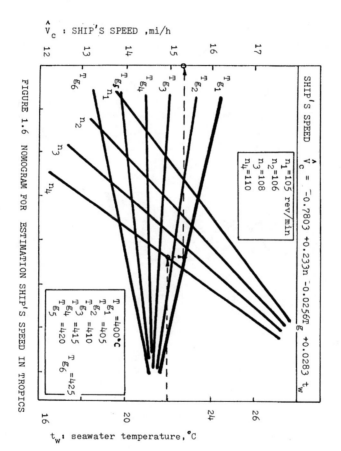

$\hat{V}_c$: SHIP'S SPEED ,mi/h

SHIP'S SPEED $\hat{V}_c = -0.7803 + 0.233n - 0.0256T_g + 0.0283\ t_w$

$n_1 = 105$ rev/min
$n_2 = 106$
$n_3 = 108$
$n_4 = 110$

$T_{g_1} = 400°C$
$T_{g_2} = 405$
$T_{g_3} = 410$
$T_{g_4} = 415$
$T_{g_5} = 420$
$T_{g_6} = 425$

t_w: seawater temperature, °C

FIGURE 1.6 NOMOGRAM FOR ESTIMATION SHIP'S SPEED IN TROPICS

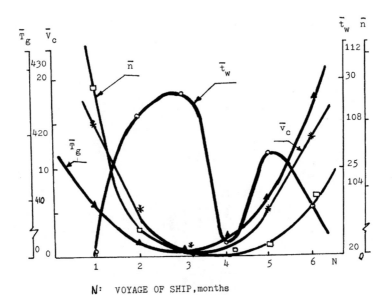

$\mathbf{N}$: VOYAGE OF SHIP, months

FIGURE 1.7 GRAPHICS OF CHANGING SHIP'S SPEED AND SOME
PARAMETERS IN TROPICS

observed data:

 □ -engine speed($\bar{n}$), rev/min

 o -seawater ($\bar{t}_w$), °C

 ▲ -exhaust temperature ($\bar{T}_g$), °C

 ＊ - ship's speed ($\bar{V}_c$) , mi/h

References

1. Perakis Inozu, "Statistical Analysis of Failure Time Distributions for Great Lakes Marine Diesels Using Censored Data," *Journal of Ship Research*, (March 1991): 73.

2. V. V. Zvonkov, "Marine Tow Tractor Calculations," (Moscow: River Transport Publisher, 1956): 51-71.

3. B.W. Parker, "Marine Transportation in Alaska's Bering Sea and Arctic Ocean Areas," *Proceedings of the First International Conference on Port and Ocean Engineering under Arctic Conditions*, (1971): 1:790-802.

4. P. Lacey and R. Edwards, "ARCO Tanker Slamming Study," *Marine Technology*, (July 1993): 135-147.

5. Eugene A. Avallone and Theodore Baumeister III, *Mark's Standard Handbook for Mechanical Engineers*, (New York: McGraw-Hill Book Company, 1987): 11-50.

Bibliography

Croxton, Frederick E. and Cowden, Dudley J., *Applied General Statistics*, New York: Prentice-Hall, Inc., 1939.

Kreyszig, Erwin, *Introduction to Mathematical Statistics*, New York: John Willey & Sons, Inc., 1970.

Morrison, Donald F., *Applied Linear Statistical Methods*, Englewood Cliffs, New Jersey: Prentice-Hall, Inc., 1983.

Pfaffenberger, Roger C. and Patterson, James H., *Statistical Methods*, Homewood, Illinois: Richard D. Irwin, Inc., 1977.

PART THREE

FUNCTIONAL ANALYSIS OF THE SHIP'S SPEED REDUCTION IN WAVES
AND THE TROPICS AND SOME CHARACTERISTICS OF THE MAIN ENGINE

1. Introduction and Background

On the basis of ship observation in the Caspian and Baltic Seas as described by the author (Zvonkov, 1956), we see that the reduction of ship speed is the function of the duration of ship navigation and the conditions of sea waves. These conclusions, mainly questions regarding sea waves, were given by Lacey and Edwards in 1993 and Washio in 1994, conforming to the North Pacific and Atlantic Oceans.

In the other cold working area, such as the Antarctic Ocean and the Bering Sea, these conclusions were marked by Parker and Vossers, which indicated that the wind and waves are at their most severe (especially in wintertime) and that these factors play a prevailing role over other factors in the reduction of ship speed. These problems in the above-named papers were not discussed conformably for the ship sailing in tropical seas where the factor of duration of ship navigation had a larger role than sea waves in questions of reduction of ship speed.

2. Some Problems of Motion for a Ship in Tropical Seawaters and the Ways of Its Realization

The general problem for the ships sailing in tropical seawaters is marine fouling of the body of the ship which significantly increases the coefficient of friction resistance and relative roughness. Therefore, the total tractive resistance of the motion of the ship increases accordingly and ship's speed decreases, and these factors as a whole promote degradation of performance for the main engine. This question was given great consideration by Crosby and Balasurbramanyan only in regard to the prevention of marine fouling on the body of the ship. However, these papers did not examine deeply the functional analysis of the reasons of reductions on the ship and the work of the engine in tropical seawaters.

The author in this paper took as a basis some main objectives:

a. To discover the functional analysis of ship speed from the influence of different factors.

b. To evaluate and analyze the changes of ship speed and some parameters of the main engine by methods of mathematical statistics on the basis of data from a dry-cargo ship with the following characteristics:
   * deidveit = 10,984 ton;
   * horsepower of main engine = 8,750;
   * average ship's speed = 14.25 knots;
   * electrocapacity = 3,700 Kw;
   * running area = Black Sea, Indian Ocean, and other tropical seas.

c. To build histograms and frequency distributions for these parameters and to describe its characteristics and shapes of distributions.

    d.   To give some recommendations for research workers and navigators in the questions of improving the work of the main engine and increasing ship speed in the tropics.

3. The Functional Analysis of the Motion of the Ship

The author of this paper thinks that ship speed is the function of the multiple of independent variables such as:

$$Y = f(X_1; X_2; X_3; \ldots\ldots\ldots X_{13}) \qquad (1)$$

where,

Y = ship speed (dependent variable), miles per hour;

and independent variables such as:

X_1 = revolution per minute of the main engine;
X_2 = duration in-service time of ship, days;
X_3 = temperature of seawater of outer cooling system of the main engine, °C;
X_4 = wind speed (Beaufort wind scale);
X_5 = wind direction on the east (E), degree;
X_6 = wind direction on northeast (NE), degree;
X_7 = wind direction on southeast (SE), degree;
X_8 = wind direction on west (W), degree;
X_9= wind direction on northwest (NW), degree;
X_{10} = wind direction on southwest (SW), degree;
X_{11} = wind direction on north (N), degree;
X_{12} = wind direction on south (S), degree;
X_{13} = temperature of exhaust gases from engine, °C.

Comparative analysis of the reduction of ship speed is shown in Figure 1 which proves scientifically that in conditions of sailing a ship in tropical seawaters, prevailing factors of this reduction of ship speed is the temperature of seawater (X_3) and duration of the in-service time of the ship (X_2) and sea wave directions ($X_5 \div X_{12}$) because these factors promote an increase of the coefficient of tractive resistance and relative roughness in account of the value of marine fouling on the body of the ship.

    So the author in this paper tries to analyze the influence of different factors on variation of ship speed and to discover some characteristics of the work of the main engine of this ship sailing in tropical waters. Figure 2 shows schematically the influence of each factor on a movable ship in the sea. However, indirectly, it is possible to consider that ship speed (Y) is also the function of revolution per minute of the main engine (X_1) and has a directly proportional dependence. With the increasing revolution of the main engine, the ship speed also increases. This functional dependence will be able to be expressed by the equation:

$$Y = f_1 (X_1) \qquad (2).$$

Herewith, the mode of operation of the engine (its heat-strength) depends also on the revolution of the engine (X_1) and the temperature of seawaters (X_3). By the criterion of the normal operation of the engine in these conditions, we are able to use the ship as index of the temperature of exhaust gases from the engine (X_{13}). So it can be written by the functional equation:

$$X_{13} = f_2 (X_1; X_3) \qquad (3).$$

Analyzing the functional equations (1), (2), and (3), we see that the ship's speed (Y) is functionally joined with the above-named variables (X_1), (X_3), and (X_{13}); i.e., it has this view:

$$Y = f [(f_1 (X_1); X_2; X_4; X_5; X_6; X_7; X_8; X_9; X_{10}; X_{11}; X_{12}; f_2 (X_1; X_3)] \qquad (4).$$

The functional model in total view for the ship's speed and operation of the main engine is shown in Figure 3. In an analysis of function (4) and Figure 3, the author makes the conclusion that a ship's speed mainly for tropical seawaters is exposed to the multiple regression analysis with the use of methods and devices of mathematical statistics.

4. Sharing Analysis of Factors Having an Influence on Ship's Speed in Tropical Seawaters

It has been said above that analysis of a ship's speed is possible with the use of mathematical statistics in order to analyze and define the general factors which play an important role on changing the above-named parameters. The author suggests the method of estimating each sharing factor in evaluation of ship's speed, and this method has the following steps:

a. To determine the general independent and dependent variable of experiment:

$$X_{1i}: X_{2i}; X_{3i}; \ldots X_{ji} \text{ (independent variables)}$$
$$(i = 1, 2, 3 \ldots n; j = 1, 2, 3 \ldots k) \text{ (5)}$$

where,

n = the number of observation (rows);
k = the number of independent variables (columns);
Y_i (dependent variable).

b. To estimate summary characteristics for each column:

$$\sum_{i=1}^{n} X_{1i}; \ \sum_{i=1}^{n} X_{2i}; \ \sum_{i=1}^{n} X_{3i}; \ \ldots \ldots \sum_{i=1}^{n} X_{ki}; \text{ and } \sum_{i=1}^{n} Y_i \quad (6)$$

c. To calculate the average values of these parameters:

$$X_1 = \frac{\sum_{i=1}^{n} X_{1i}}{n}; \ X_2 = \frac{\sum_{i=1}^{n} X_{2i}}{n}; \ \ldots \ldots X_k = \frac{\sum_{i=1}^{n} X_{ki}}{n}; \text{ and } Y = \frac{\sum_{i=1}^{n} Y_i}{n}; \quad (7)$$

d. To estimate summary characteristics of independent variables for each i = value; i.e.,

$$X_{si} = \sum_{j=1}^{k} \ X_{ji} = \sum_{j=1}^{k} \ (X_{1i} + X_{2i} + \ldots X_{ki}) \quad (8)$$

$$X_{s1} = \sum_{j=1}^{k} X_{j1}; \ \ X_{s2} = \sum_{j=2}^{k} X_{j2}; \ \ldots \ldots X_{sn} = \sum_{j=1}^{k} \ X_{jn}$$

e. To calculate the average of sharing dependent variable indexes of ship's speed:

$$Y_{si} = \frac{Y_i}{X_{si}} = \frac{Y_i}{\sum_{j=1}^{k} (X_{1i} + X_{2i} + \ldots X_{j1})} \quad (9)$$

$$Y_s = \frac{\sum_{i=1}^{n}}{n} = \frac{\sum_{i=1}^{n} (Y_{s1} + Y_{s2} + \ldots Y_{sn})}{n} \quad (10)$$

f. To estimate the average percentage of sharing independent variable indexes of ship's speed:

$$\Delta X_{1i} = \frac{X_{1i}}{X_{si}} \cdot 100\% \ ;$$

$$\Delta X_{2i} = \frac{X_{2i}}{X_{si}} \cdot 100\% \ ;$$

- -

$$\Delta X_{ki} = \frac{X_{ki}}{X_{si}} \cdot 100\% \ ;$$

and

$$\Delta \bar{X}_1 = \frac{\sum_{i=1}^{n} \Delta X_{1i}}{n} ;$$

$$\Delta \bar{X}_2 = \frac{\sum_{i=1}^{n} \Delta X_{2i}}{n} ;$$

$$------------------$$

$$\Delta \bar{X}_k = \frac{\sum_{i=1}^{n} \Delta X_{ki}}{n} ;$$

In Table 1.1 an example indicates that the average percent of sharing indexes are joined functionally with ship's speed ($\bar{Y} = 6.08$ knots is the average ship's speed accepted as 100 percent).

Table 1.1
Calculation of sharing percent indexes are joined functionally with ship's speed.

$\Delta\bar{X}_1$	$\Delta\bar{X}_2$	$\Delta\bar{X}_3$	$\Delta\bar{X}_4$	$\Delta\bar{X}_5$	$\Delta\bar{X}_6$	$\Delta\bar{X}_7$	$\Delta\bar{X}_8$	$\Delta\bar{X}_9$	$\Delta\bar{X}_{10}$	$\Delta\bar{X}_{11}$	$\Delta\bar{X}_{12}$	$\Delta\bar{X}_{13}$
6.02	42.09	13.93	0.16	8.11	0.23	2.23	0.74	0.44	0.71	0.40	1.42	23.47

Figure 4 shows a characteristic of each parameter functionally influencing a ship's speed. Analysis of Figure 4 indicates the one fact that most influences the reduction of a ship's speed is the duration of in-service time of a ship (X_2); the sharing percent index is joined functionally with the ship's speed and is equal to $\Delta \bar{X}_2 = 42.09$ percent, and particularly this is important for the ship sailing in tropical seawaters than in cold seawaters. Not the least of the factors is the temperature of exhaust gases from the engine (X_{13}) and the temperature of seawater inputting in the engine as an outer cooling system (X_3); i.e., the operation process of the main engine, because the sharing indexes functionally influencing on the ship's speed accordingly are equal to $\Delta \bar{X}_3 = 13.98$ percent and $\Delta \bar{X}_{13} = 23.47$ percent.

5. The Peculiarities of Operation of the Main Engine and Motion of the Ship in Tropical Seawaters

Characteristic peculiarities of the operation of the main engine and a ship in the conditions of sailing in the tropics becomes more obvious. First of all, because with the duration of in-service time of a ship, the revolution of the engine and the ship's speed decrease accordingly (Figure 5). In analyzing Figure 5 we see for the period in which ships are sailing in tropical seawaters for more than six months, the average revolution of the main engine decreases more than 6 percent in comparison with its starting value of $n = 110$ revolutions per min.

Otherwise leaving the revolution of the main engine constant for the duration of the whole trip will raise the temperature of the exhaust gases from the engine; i.e., the heat-stress of the engine will increase, and the service life of the engine will decrease as a result of this action. Therefore, in practical conditions for the ships sailing in tropical seawaters, one should periodically correct the revolution of the main engine until the value of the present temperature of exhaust gases will be normal in the working processes of the main engine. The process of correcting the revolution of the main engine is shown in Figure 6 as a process of sailing a ship in the tropics for a period more than six months.

6. Statistical Analysis of General Parameters of Motion of the Ship and Operation of the Main Engine

Analyzing Figure 4, we see the duration of in-service time of the ship (X_2) is the most important factor of decreasing the ship speed. A characteristic peculiarity of the histogram and expected distribution (Figure 7) of this parameter (X_2) shows that the frequency is equal to $f = 1$, relative frequency is equal to $P(x) = 0.0055$, and percentage of frequency is equal to $\hat{p} = 0.55$ percent. This will characterize the histogram distribution as discrete (rectangular) symmetric distribution with the following characteristics:

Mean:

$$E(X_2) = \sum_{i=1}^{n} X_2\, P(x) = \sum_{i=1}^{n} X_2(1/n) = (1/n) \sum_{i=1}^{n} X_2 \tag{13}$$

where,

n = the number of observations;
Variance:

$$V(X_2) = \sum_{i=1}^{n} [X_2 - E(X_2)]^2\, P(x) = (1/n) \sum_{i=1}^{n} [X_2 - E(X_2)]^2 \tag{14}$$

It is necessary to admit that the equally important characteristic in the evaluation of the ship's motion is the regime of operation of the main engine, namely, as the revolution of engine (X_1) examined above in Figure 6 and the temperature of exhaust gases (X_{13}) from the main engine. The histogram and expected distribution of parameter is shown in Figure 8. Analysis of the histogram and expected distributions as shown in Figures 6 and 8 indicates the similarity of their distributions. In both cases, the character of these distributions submits to the rules of positive skewed right distribution with the parameters:

$$g_1 = \frac{3(X_{j*} - Mdn)}{\sigma} \tag{15}$$

where,

g_1 = skewness;

$\bar{X}_{j\cdot}$ = the arithmetical mean from grouped data $(j = 1, 2, 3 \ldots n)$, equal

$$\bar{X}_{j\cdot} = \frac{\bar{X}_d + \Sigma\, fd}{n} \qquad (16)$$

$\bar{X}_d$ = the selected mid-value of any class;

d = deviation from assumed mean;

σ = standard deviation, grouped data, equal

$$\sigma = \sqrt{\frac{\Sigma\, f\, x_i^{\,2}}{n}} \qquad (17)$$

where,

x_i = deviation of mid-values i-class from $\bar{X}_{j\cdot}$, equal

$$x_i = (\bar{X}_d - \bar{X}_{j\cdot}) \qquad (18).$$

Analysis of Figure 6 and Figure 8 shows that their distributions have peaked more than normal, and, for this reason, such distribution will be referred to as the leptokurtic distribution with estimation parameter such as kurtosis:

$$g_2 = \frac{\Sigma\, f\, x^4}{n\, \sigma^{\,4}} \qquad (19).$$

Conformably to Figure 6 we have the following:

$\bar{X}_d = 50; \Sigma\, fd = 979; n = 183; \bar{X}_{1\cdot} = 55.35; \Sigma\, fx^2 = 4.42 \bullet 10^5; \Sigma\, fx^4 = 1.08 \bullet 10^9;$
$\sigma = 49.15; Mdn = 44.50; g_{1_1} = 0.66; g_{2_1} = 1.01.$

Conformably to Figure 8 we have the following:

$\bar{X}_d = 207; \Sigma\, fd = 2162; n = 183; \bar{X}_{13\cdot} = 218.81; \Sigma\, fx^2 = 7.02 \bullet 10^6; \Sigma\, fx^4 = 2.797 \bullet 10^{11};$
$= 195.90; Mdn = 184; g_{1_{13}} = 0.53; g_{2_{13}} = 1.89.$

From Figure 6 we see that the greater percentage of frequency of distribution ($\hat{p}$ = 49.7 percent) falls on the period of mooring the ship in the harbor with tropical seawaters (the revolution of the main engine in this period was equal to zero). As a result of these actions, the body of the ship was encrusted significantly with marine growth.

The same picture has been placed on Figure 8, where it shows the intercommunication of temperatures of the exhaust gases from the revolution of the main engine. With decreasing revolution (X_1) of the engine, the temperature of exhaust gases (X_{13}) increase accordingly. As was shown above, the temperature of seawater indirectly influences the changing of ship speed and operation of the main engines, therefore, the studying of this parameter deserves more attention.

Figure 9 shows the histogram and view of the expected distribution of this parameter (X_3). Analysis of Figure 9 shows that the shape of the frequency distribution is bimodal, consisting of two peaks at this complex distribution, which has generalized the characteristics:

*The average value	$\overline{X}_{w_3} = 24.30$;
*Mode	$\overline{M}_{w_3} = 25$;
*Median	$\overline{Mdn}_{w_3} = 22.36$;
*Coefficient of variation	$\overline{CV}_{w_3} = 11.57$ percent;
*Standard deviation	$\overline{S.D}_{w_3} = 4.69$;
*Skewness	$\overline{g_1}_3 = 0$;
*Kurtosis	$\overline{g_2}_3 = 2.07$.

As the value of skewness is equal to $\overline{g_1}_3 = 0$, analysis of Figure 9 indicates that the symmetric distribution and the value of kurtosis is equal to $\overline{g_2}_3 = 2.07$ and indicates on the considerable flat of the curve of polygon distribution on the side of the right part of this distribution.

So the author of this paper investigates, on the basis of statistical analysis, three general characteristics which influence the operation of the main engine:

a. The revolution per minute of the engine;
b. The temperature of exhaust gases from the engine;
c. The temperature of seawaters in the tropics;

All these parameters were described and shown in Figure 6 and Figure 8, which have abnormal distribution with the positive right-side-skewed and bimodal distribution shown and described in Figure 9 with two peaks. Variation of ship speed for the period of duration of in-service time of the ship is shown in Figure 10.

Analysis of Figure 10 with expected distribution and the histogram shows that the percentage of frequency is equal to $\hat{p} = 49.7$ percent and falls in the period of the ship standing in the harbor, and the average ship's speed was equal to $\overline{Y}_s = 10.95$ knots for the period of motion with a percentage frequency equal to $\hat{p} = 27.8$ percent. Analysis of Figure 10 also shows that the ship's speed significantly decreases in the period of sailing the ship in tropical seawaters, particularly after the ship was standing in the harbor.

And besides, analysis of Figure 10 also shows that the shape of frequency in data is distributed as abnormal distribution and has a U-shaped distribution, as the extreme values have the highest frequencies and fewer values are in the center, which have the total characteristics of this distribution:

*The average value $\overline{X_{w_y}}$ = 8.42;

*Mode $\overline{M_{w_y}}$ = 6.7;

*Coefficient of variance $\overline{CV_{w_y}}$ = 43.45 percent;

*Standard deviation $\overline{S.D._{w_y}}$ = 6.17;

*Skewness $\overline{g1_y}$ = 0.06;

*Kurtosis $\overline{g2_y}$ = 0.525.

Therefore, from Figure 10 we see that the ship's speed during sailing in the tropics has an abnormal distribution and the frequency polygon has the complex U-shaped distribution. Besides the other factors, the most important role in reduction of ship speed is the wind speed and its directions on the ship during motion on the sea. That fact is shown in the histogram and expected distribution of these indexes as in Figure 11 and Figure 12. Analysis of the expected distribution as shown in Figure 11 indicates that its curves has an abnormal distribution with positive right skewness in the following parameters:

*The average value $\overline{X_4}$ = 3.14;

*Mode $\overline{M_4}$ = 1;

*Standard deviation σ_4 = 0.62;

*Coefficient of variation $\overline{CV_4}$ = 19.75 percent;

*Skewness $\overline{g1_4}$ = 1.04;

*Kurtosis $\overline{g2_4}$ = 24.5

As the value of kurtosis is equal to $\overline{g2_4}$ = 24.5 > 3, this is indicated on a most considerable peaked curve of this distribution and the value of skewness is equal to $\overline{g1_4}$ = 1.04; this characterizes a slight positive skew. The histogram and expected distribution of the data of wind speed are shown in Figure 12, which holds a significant influence on reduction of ship speed and operation of the main engine. As we see from Figure 12, extreme values reach the right side of this distribution, and all this shows that the frequency of the polygon relates to a J-shaped distribution in the following parameters:

*The average value $\overline{X_{5\div12}}$ = 202.5;

*Mode $\overline{M_{5\div12}}$ = 360;

*Standard deviation $\sigma_{5\div12}$ = 31.51;

*Coefficient of variation $\overline{CV_{5\div12}}$ = 15.56 percent;

*Skewness $\overline{g1_{5\div12}}$ = 0.015;

*Kurtosis $\overline{g2_{5\div12}}$ = -2.77.

The negative value of skewness ($\overline{g}_{15\div12}$ = - 0.015) indicates a slight negative skew, and the value of kurtosis is equal to g_2 = - 2.77; this indicates a slightly platykurtic distribution. Statistical analysis of ship speed and some characteristics of the main engine are shown in above-named Figures 6, 7, 8, 9, 10, 11, and 12, allowing the following conclusions:

a.   Positive skewed right distributions have such functional parameters as:
        *revolution of the main engine (Figure 6);
        *temperature of exhaust gases from the engine (Figure 8);
        *wind speed (Figure 11).

b.   Bimodal distribution has such parameters as:
        *temperature of tropical seawater (Figure 9).

c.   U-shaped distribution has such parameters as:
        *variation of the average ship speed during sailing of the ship in tropical seawaters (Figure 10).

d.   J-shaped distribution has such parameters as:
        *direction of wind speed on the moving ship in the sea (Figure 12).

e.   Discrete (rectangular) distribution has such parameters as:
        *duration of in-service time of the ship (Figure 7).

7. Conclusions and Recommendations

a.   The main objective of this paper was focused on statistical analysis of ship speed reduction in conditions of sailing the ship in tropical seawaters. General attention was devoted to the functional analysis of parameters influencing the ship's speed and also to the operation of the main engine.

b.   The results of the paper are shown in view of histograms and expected distributions for each variable parameter, indicating the most important characteristics of these distributions in a generalized view.

c.   The statistical analysis indicates that the ship speed, after six months of sailing in tropical seawaters, has a 30 percent reduction from the starting ship's speed. This reduction of ship speed was reached by means of duration of the in-service time of the ship (more than six months of sailing in the tropical seawaters). An indirect index of this event is in the reduction of ship speed as a result of marine fouling on the body of this ship.

d. A similar picture focused on the main engine indicates that the revolution of the engine decreases to 6 percent in analogical conditions.

The author in this paper gave some recommendations about improving the operation of the main engine and increasing the ship speed in the process of sailing ships in tropical seawaters such as:

(1) To put into additional operation every six months according to the priority of the presentation and the arrangement of ships in dock for removing of marine fouling from the body of the ship constantly sailing in tropical seawaters.

(2) To design a more effective outer cooling system for the main engine than the present one is using for cooling seawater until the temperature is in limits of $15 \div 20°C$ for decreasing heat-stress and improving the operation of the engine.

(3) As a result, the rising temperature of exhaust gases in the same revolutions of the engine is an indirect index of marine fouling on the body of the ship, and these peculiarities must be included in service duties for motorists or mechanics of these ships.

(4) To do a correction of revolutions of the main engine in time depending on recommendations to maintain the temperature of the exhaust gases of the engine in normal conditions (each engine has a normal level of this grade accordingly with recommendations of the manufacturing company).

(5) To investigate and evaluate the proposed conclusions and recommendations of the author of this paper on the other ships sailing mainly in the tropics and to design later the universal recommendations in view of the standard document for these ships.

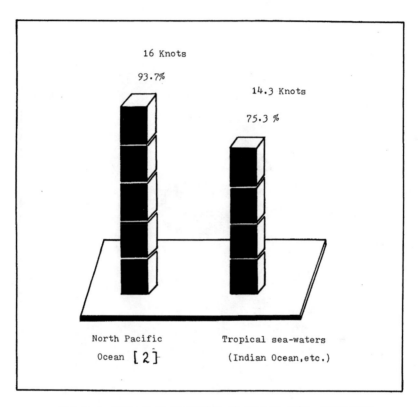

16 Knots

93.7%

14.3 Knots

75.3 %

North Pacific
Ocean [2]

Tropical sea-waters
(Indian Ocean,etc.)

Figure 1 Percent in reduction of average ship speed from
primary motion of ship in different sea-waters
with duration of service time over 6 months.

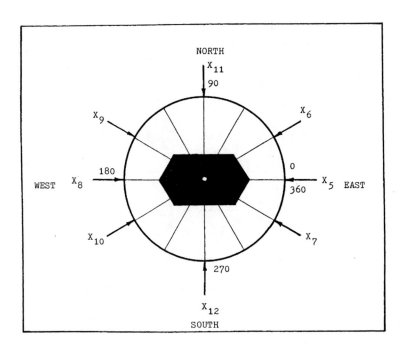

Figure 2   Possible direction of wind speed on movable

ship in sea-waters.

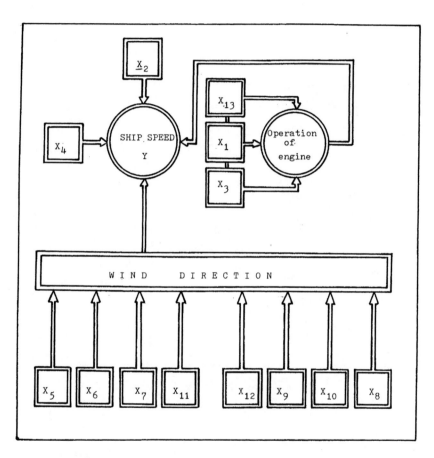

Figure 3   Functional model of ship speed and operation of
main engine.

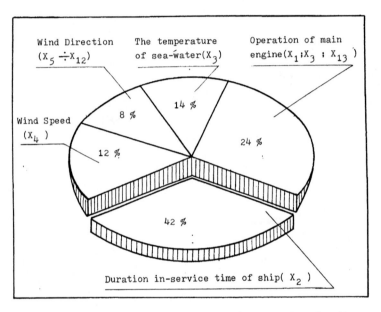

Figure 4 General components of sharing indexes functionally
influenced by ship speed.

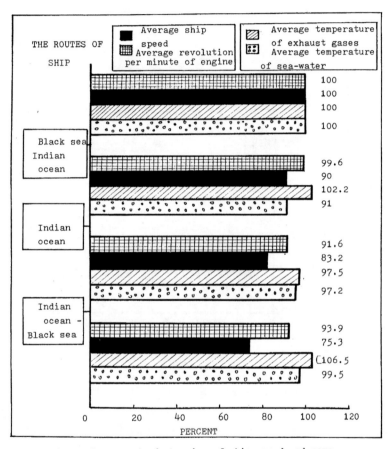

Figure 5 Percent of changing of ship speed and some
characteristics of the main engine in the tropics.
(period of sailing : August–January)

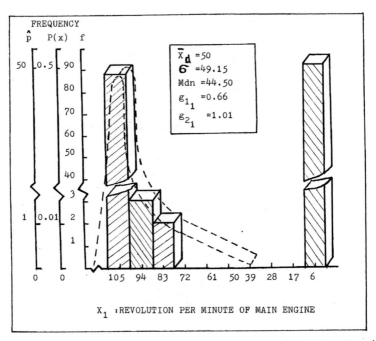

Figure 6 Histogram and expected distribution(hidden line)
of revolution of the main engine (X_1) with
relative P(x),percentage ($\hat{p}$) and frequency (f)
axes.

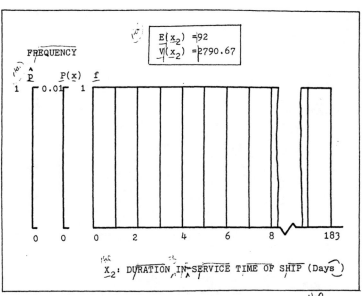

Figure 7 Histogram of duration in-service time (X_2) of ship with relative P (x) percentage ($\hat{p}$) and frequency (f) axes.

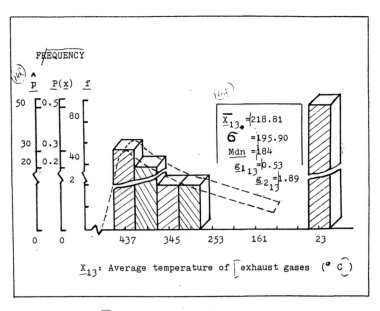

Figure 8 Histogram and expected distribution (hidden
line) of the average temperature of exhaust
gases (X_{13}) from the main engine with relative
$P(x)$, percentage ($\hat{p}$), and frequency (f) axes.

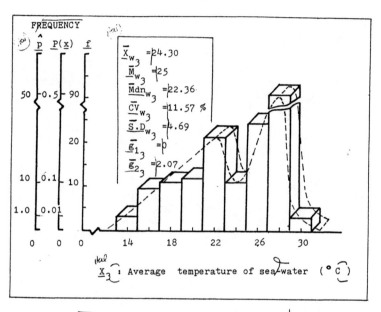

FREQUENCY

$\overline{X}_{w_3}$ = 24.30

$\overline{M}_{w_3}$ = 25

$\overline{Mdn}_{w_3}$ = 22.36

$\overline{CV}_{w_3}$ = 11.57 %

$\overline{S.D}_{w_3}$ = 4.69

$\overline{g_1}_3$ = 0

$\overline{g_2}_3$ = 2.07

$\underline{X}_3$: Average temperature of sea water (°C)

Figure 9 Histogram and expected distribution (hidden line) of the average temperature of sea waters ($\underline{X}_3$) with relative P(x), percentage (p) and frequency (f) axes.

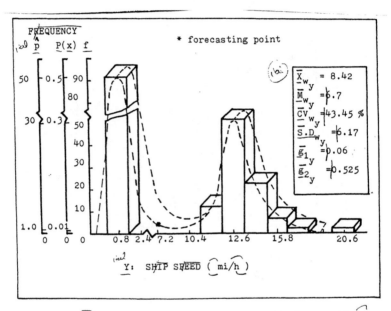

Figure 10 Histogram and expected distribution (hidden line)
of the average ship speed (Y) with relative P(x),
percentage (p) and frequency (f) axes.

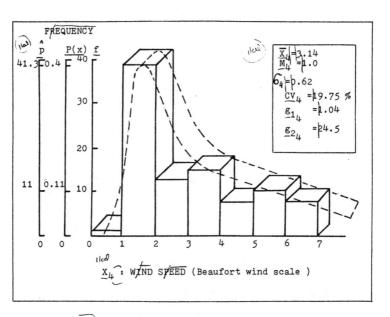

FREQUENCY

$\overline{X}_4 = 3.14$
$\underline{M}_4 = 1.0$
$\hat{6}_4 = 0.62$
$\underline{CV}_4 = 19.75 \%$
$\underline{g1}_4 = 1.04$
$\underline{g2}_4 = 24.5$

$\underline{X}_4$: WIND SPEED (Beaufort wind scale)

Figure 11   Histogram and expected distribution of wind
speed ($\underline{X}_4$) with relative $\underline{P}(x)$, percentage ($\hat{\underline{p}}$) and
frequency ($\underline{f}$) axes.

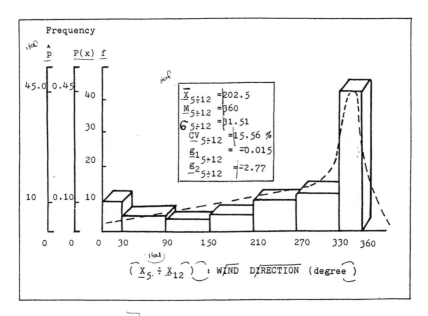

Figure 12 ⌐ Histogram and expected distribution (hidden line) of direction of wind ($\underline{X}_5 \div \underline{X}_{12}$) with relative $\underline{P(x)}$ percentage ($\underline{p}$) and frequency ($\underline{f}$) axes.

References

1. V. V. Zvonkov, "Marine Tow Tractor Calculations," (Moscow: River Transport Publisher, 1956): 51-71.

2. P. Lacey and R. Edwards, "ARCO Tanker Slamming Study," *Marine Technology*, (July 1993): 135-147.

3. Y. Washio, M. Miyoshi, K. Takekuma, K. Vamada, and K. Kobayashi, "Recent Research and Development in the Design of an Oceanographic Research Vessel," *Marine Technology*, (January 1994): 1-19.

4. B. W. Parker, "Marine Transportation in Alaska's Bering Sea and Arctic Ocean Areas," *Proceedings of the First International Conference on Port and Ocean Engineering under Arctic Conditions*, (Trondheim, Norway: Technical University of Norway, 1972), 1: 790-802.

5. G. Vossers, *Resistance, Propulsion and Steering of Ships*, (Antwerp-Cologne:The Technical Publishing Company H. Stam N.V. Haarlem, 1962), 11C: 83.

6. R. M. Crosby, "Ocean Instrumentation: The Better Use of Materials Technology," *1970 IEEE International Conference on Engineering in the Ocean Environment*, (September 1970): 147-149.

7. R. Balasurbramanyan, N. Unnikrishnan Nair, and A. G. Gopalakrishna Pellai, "The Problem of Marine Fouling in the Coastal Waters of India and Its Economic Implications with Special Reference to Fishing Fleet Management," *Proceedings: Third International Congress on Marine Corrosion and Fouling*, (Evanston, Illinois: Northwestern University Press, 1972): 898.

8. J. Sandison, D. Woolaver, M. Dipper, and M. Rice, "Sea Trials of the SWATH Ship USNS Victorious (T-AGOS 19)," *Marine Technology*, (October 1994), 31: 245-257.

Bibliography

Croxton, Frederick E. and Cowden, Dudley J., *Applied General Statistics*, New York: Prentice-Hall, Inc., 1939.

Havilcek, L. L. and Crain, R. D., *Practical Statistics for the Physical Sciences*, Washington, D.C.: American Chemical Society, 1988.

Heywood, John B., *Internal Combustion Engine Fundamentals*, New York: McGraw-Hill Book Company, 1988.

Kreyszig, Erwin, *Introductory Mathematical Statistics*, New York: John Wiley & Sons, 1970.

Meyer, Stuart L., *Data Analysis for Scientists and Engineers*, New York: John Wiley & Sons, 1975.

Pfaffenberger, Roger C. and Patterson, James H., *Statistical Methods*, Homewood, Illinois: Richard D. Irwin, Inc., 1977.

Schmid, Calvin F., *Statistical Graphics*, New York: John Wiley & Sons, 1983.